LEADERSHIP EVERY DAY

How to Lead Others Efficiently and Effectively

ALAN WEISS, PH.D.

author of
Our Emperors Have No Clothes

LEADERSHIP EVERY DAY

How to Lead Others Efficiently and Effectively

ALAN WEISS, PH.D.

Las Brisas Research Press

Printed in the United States of America

Published by Las Brisas Research Press, East Greenwich, RI

ISBN 1-886158-05-3

Table of Contents

Introduction

There are 57 different keys for leadership which you will learn by the end of this brief book. Apply just one and you'll be more effective tomorrow than you are today.

This book was written as a result of my firm's work in leadership with major organizations around the country and around the world. My fifth book, *Our Emperors Have No Clothes*, deals with the lack of leadership that has plagued many organizations. This booklet focuses on both the art and science of leadership, and how to become more adept at both.

Leadership used to be based primarily upon control and power. The control was derived from the "possession" of people and information, and the power from the ability to reward and punish. Viewed more positively, the leader was a "hero," who provided direction and support for those who followed. He or she could be relied upon to provide answers and solutions for those who would implement. In harsh environments the leader was militaristic and authoritarian, and in kind environments the leader was parental and nurturing.

Today, of course, the traditional sources of power have evaporated. Organizations are leaner and much more dependent upon technology than physical labor. Thus, the number of "bodies" controlled no longer denotes power. Nor, for that matter, does information, since everyone has access to a computer on the desk, over the phone and from the briefcase. Finally, reward and punishment are often illusory in times of decreased loyalty, fewer opportunities for upward mobility, and an accent on teams rather than individual contributions.

This booklet was written with the new leader—the "post-heroic" leader—in mind. Leadership is more crucial than ever before, but its practice and application are significantly different from former paradigms. This is the first time that we have provided these practices and principles in an inexpensive, easily-accessible medium.

Because people learn in different ways, and some readers may find certain ideas more useful than others, the book is designed with three learning alternatives, each intended to provide flexibility toward retaining and applying whatever is relevant to you:

① There is a subject heading and action summary on each even-numbered page, to allow for quick reference and easy scanning.

② There are detailed examples and guidelines on the odd-numbered pages to allow for highlighting and more comprehensive support.

③ There are three "keys" provided with each chapter which constitute immediate action points to help implement the ideas presented.

There are *57 different keys* for leadership that you will review by the end of this booklet, covering *19 different areas* which support effective and efficient leadership. How many will apply to you? That's a matter of personal volition and intent. But remember our credo throughout this professional development series of booklets: Improve by 1% a day, and in 70 days you're twice as productive as you were at the outset. It sounds easy, but few people achieve it.

I've tried to provide the most important attributes, behaviors and skills I've found in the best leaders I've observed. Adopt one, or apply them all. All you need is that 1% improvement every day.

— Alan Weiss, Ph.D.
East Greenwich, Rhode Island

Speak Through Your Actions

Ride Into Battle at the Head of Your Troops

People will only "hear" what they "see." First and foremost, leaders are exemplars. "Do as I say, not as I do" is the certain sign of a fraud.

THREE KEYS:

1. Demonstrate—exemplify—your intent at the first opportunity after expressing it.
2. When there are exceptions, explain the rationale. But remember that too many exceptions will destroy the intent.
3. Examine your own workplace behavior, and ask if you would be happy and successful if all of your people emulated it.

"Your actions are so loud, I can't hear what you're saying," observed Ralph Waldo Emerson. Every time that a leader sends a message, he or she is providing two messages: One is the content (what the leader wants done) and the other is the process or style (how the leader conveys it). The latter is at least as important as the former, because it provides the cultural context for the recipients.

No matter what the nature of your organization, no one in it believes what they see and hear. They only believe what they see. There is no more powerful shaper of behavior in the organization than the behaviors of those in leadership positions. **Above all else, the leader is an exemplar.**

I've been in countless organizations which post their "values" on every available square foot of wall space. Inevitably, near the top of the list is a statement about respect and equitable treatment for employees. Yet in many of these organizations, employees can see colleagues being brutally treated right beneath the laminated plaques. As one supervisor noted, "You can treat people ruthlessly here, as long as you make your numbers." That cultural reality immediately destroys every plaque, banner and button in the company.

Leaders establish the behavioral realities of the workplace. Above all else, they establish and embody the real values of the organization and, by extension, its relationships with customers, suppliers and partners. In over two decades of consulting, I've never observed an organization—public or private—which had unhappy employees and happy customers. If leaders provide the message that the customer is a necessary evil and general bother, employees will usually reflect that in minimum service, lack of courtesy and zero initiative. If leaders demonstrate in their own actions that customers are the number one priority (i.e., leaving an internal meeting because a customer is on the phone), employees will reflect that in innovative service and proactive contact.

Which of these sets of behaviors are you exemplifying?

• Accessible and responsive	• Screened behind secretaries
• Action-oriented	• Equivocating
• Accepting prudent risks	• Accepting only the ultra-safe course
• Beliefs reflected in behaviors	• Beliefs solely in memos and directives
• Accepting accountability	• Avoiding accountability
• Investing others with trust	• Cynical and trusting of no one
• Sharing credit and victories	• Allowing no one else in the limelight
• Allowing the freedom to fail	• Threatening those who don't succeed
• Developing others	• Every person for themselves

In modern warfare, generals sit in rear command posts and order troops into battle. During the Civil War, generals mounted their horses, making them the most obvious targets on the battlefield, and led their troops into the battle.

We need leaders who ride into battle at the head of their troops.

Paint A Picture of the Future
Use Bold Strokes and Vivid Colors

Today's decisions should be guided by tomorrow's needs, not yesterday's habits. Help people to visualize the direction of the enterprise.

THREE KEYS:

1. An overemphasis on "how" will create a direction by default. Help everyone to understand the "what." You cannot set a proper course unless you know the port to which you're heading.
2. Make the future as concrete and tangible as possible, even if you have to periodically amend it. Ambiguity will result in differing views by different decision makers.
3. Don't hesitate to change course. You might envision a better port, or see a storm approaching on the current heading for the existing port. Let people know the rationale, though, so they can adjust their decisions.

Organizations make or lose money every day, not by decisions made in the executive suite, but by the thousands of decisions made by employees throughout the organization. These decisions—providing discounts, accepting returns, selecting suppliers, creating inventories, and so on—should be made in concert with the decisions being made across the hall, down the stairs and around the country (or world). Ideally, everyone needs to be looking at the same picture of the future.

The philosopher Santayana defined a fanatic as "someone who loses sight of the goal, and consequently redoubles efforts to achieve it." In other words, if we don't know the port-of-call, no wind is favorable. Leaders provide as clear a picture of the future as possible, clarifying ambiguity and painting in as much detail as is known. That picture of the future becomes the template that employees can use to guide their daily decision making. Is this supplier consistent with that quality goal? Does this policy with customers help us to achieve that market penetration? Will this pricing policy help us to achieve the image we're seeking?

Are you creating a picture—a vision—of the future that is communicated and relevant to employees? Are you painting in colors, or only in black and white? Is your canvass large enough to support the details and scope, and provide true perspective?

Without a vision of the company's future, people will focus on what the company is today. Their decisions and actions will perpetuate the current state of affairs or, worse, yesterday's state of affairs. We have consistently observed organizations doing a fine job of training, educating and developing their people to meet yesterday's needs when they should be focused on tomorrow's realities. The training function shouldn't be painting that picture. Leadership should.

Frequently, organizations pursue a direction that has been established by default. The lack of a clear vision and strategy means that every wind and tide will affect the course, and competitors, economic conditions, governmental regulations and societal trends will all exert their influence. As employees perceive these events in varying ways, their consequent decisions will vary accordingly, creating conflicts and confusion in the operation. Instead of a clear picture, everyone is viewing a changing kaleidoscope, interpreting the colors and the shapes as best they can.

The attributes of a clear vision should include:

- What the enterprise will look like, structurally.
- How it will interact with its customers.
- What its primary goals and measures of success will be.
- How it will interact internally.
- Which performance measures will be most valued.
- How performers can best contribute to the goals.

In other words, where are we going, how will we get there, how will we know that we're making progress, and what is our role during the journey? Paint with bold strokes and vivid colors. If you make a mistake, correct it. Even da Vinci was constantly improving what was on his canvas.

Align Individual and Organizational Goals

Focus and Fine Tune the Picture

Individual self-interest should be compatible with organizational direction. If I'm rewarded for avoiding risk, I'm not going to be very innovative.

THREE KEYS:

1. Establish positive consequences for the behaviors which support organizational direction, and negative consequences for those which do not.
2. Translate organizational goals so that they are meaningful in the daily accountabilities of the employee.
3. Reexamine goals as frequently as quarterly. There is nothing magical (or safe) about annual reviews in times of accelerating change.

Even perfect organizational goals are valueless if they aren't translated into tangible, clear and acceptable individual goals. This is often called "alignment," meaning that the leader must ensure that the individual is focused on, evaluated and rewarded for the production of results which support the overall direction of the enterprise. Such congruence does not occur automatically. In fact, it's fairly common to observe employees performing very ably in pursuit of individual goals which are actually antithetical to the organization's goals. That is not an employee failure, it's a leadership failure.

In the graphic on the left, you can see that the achievement of the organization's vision follows concurrent and mutually-supportive paths. On the left is the operational path, which identifies results and consequent tasks to reach goals. On the right is the cultural/behavioral path, which identifies how people must act in order to achieve the goals.

The left might be termed the "core or strategic belief system," and the right the "operating belief system." No one outside of the executive suite is especially motivated, for example, by the (quite legitimate) corporate goal of increasing shareholder value. In fact, it's difficult to quickly determine if one's actions at any given moment are contributing to that end. It's up to leadership to *translate* that goal into an operating reality, with the appropriate support and consequences. A bank branch manager would be enhancing shareholder value if he or she emphasized the rollover of retirement funds, for example, and the tellers would understand that their reminding customers of new savings instrument rates was important for the branch.

The steps in alignment for the leader:

- Identify and articulate corporate vision.
- Identify and describe key business goals.
- Identify and define key operating values.
- Establish agreement on tactics needed.
- Establish agreement on behaviors required.
- Jointly establish performance goals.
- Jointly measure results.
- Balance the rewards to reflect progress on both paths.

Leaders keep the overall picture in focus by understanding that people view it through various filters and lenses. Fine tuning is required if we are all to see the same future and understand our roles in achieving it.

Develop People to Within an Inch of their Lives

You Train Animals, You Educate People

Every manager is the human resources manager. At the end of the day, if you haven't helped others improve at what they do, you've wasted your time.

THREE KEYS:

1. Develop skills and abilities by providing knowledge and expertise.
2. Develop wisdom by providing experiences and the freedom to fail.
3. Develop "street smarts" and cultural adeptness through mentoring.

The poet Maya Angelou observed that you train animals but you educate people. That distinction applies to our workplace more than anywhere else. Every day—in fact, right now, as you read this—organizations are wasting money by providing too much training and not enough educating. Training provides for the learning of tasks, i.e., how to use a lathe, how to fill out a form, how to access files on the computer. But education provides for the use of one's intelligence, focusing on the *why* of the job: you're building a fine piece of furniture, helping someone obtain insurance benefits, determining our perception among customers.

When people are educated about the reason for the job, they are enabled to use their judgment, intellect and talents to achieve the proper end. When they are simply taught how to do an arbitrary task, they can only fix whatever gets in the way of their task. People in the latter condition are most often heard to state, "Sorry, that's not my job," when asked to deviate an inch from their routine.

One of the fundamental roles of the "post-heroic" leader is to develop people, to help them work smarter and not harder. This is especially critical in our increasingly information-bound organizations.

There are three major areas of development for the leader to support:

1. Providing the skills and abilities required. This is best accomplished by ensuring that people have access to the knowledge and expertise required to do the job. Skills-building generally requires understanding of the demands, practice with the skills, application of the skills, and feedback on performance.

2. Developing the wisdom required to perform the job. This includes modifying behaviors to best suit the interpersonal demands of the job, providing experience and the ability to make one's own mistakes in learning (the "freedom to fail"), and the ongoing communication that supports successes and provides learning from setbacks.

3. Inculcating the "street smarts," organizational mores and cultural realities of the environment. Most organizations have more unwritten rules than written ones, and adherence to the cultural norms is important to one's success.

This is the essence of the mentoring process, and every leader should be serving as mentor to several people at any given time. (One of the problems in fostering multiculturalism in organizations is that those in the best position to be mentors are often white males, and many of those who can best benefit from mentoring are females and minorities. White males must assertively seek mentorees *unlike* themselves, and minorities and women must actively seek out mentors unlike themselves.)

"Human resource development" is not an abstract that floats around the periphery of the organization, nor is it a technical necessity residing in the basement office of an obscure specialist. *Every* manager is a human resources manager, and *every* leader is accountable for the effort.

Dogs are noble animals, and very good, presumably, at being dogs. If you treat them like people, you tend to ruin them as dogs. You'll no less ruin your people by treating them like dogs.

Focus Overwhelmingly On Results

The Customer's Opinion Is the Only One that Matters

Tasks and inputs are important to the quality of the output. However, when we measure only the input and consume ourselves with the task, the output suffers. Bureaucracy is the triumph of means over ends.

THREE KEYS:

1. Maximize the resources, focus and measurements devoted to the customer and use of the product and service.
2. Minimize internal disruption and internal disrupters which deflect the energy required to focus externally.
3. Abandon any quality movement or program which does not have an impact on the customer. If the customer doesn't feel it, it doesn't exist.

M

Dogs are noble animals, and very good, presumably, at being dogs. If you treat them like people, you tend to ruin them as dogs. You'll no less ruin your people by treating them like dogs.

Most organizations I've observed are highly competent at metrics. They can measure performance to the fifth decimal, measure volumes in five different classifications, and create comparative statistics which accurately compare efforts in any given time period. A great deal of leadership time is invested in the generation, analysis and evaluation of these measures. They are comforting, and provide an aura of control.

The problem, of course, is that most organizations are measuring the wrong things.

Every organization possesses only 100% of the sum total of its people's talents and energies. Despite the calls for "doing more with less" and "giving 110%," the immutable fact of the matter is, add everything together, and you get 100%. The key for leadership *is in the ultimate aim of that investment.*

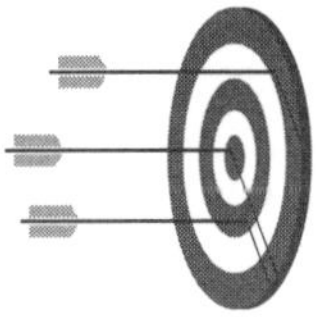

Leaders maximize the resources directed *externally*, at the customer, and the customer's use of the products and services of the enterprise. They minimize the energy directed *internally*, at office politics, feelings of unfair treatment, reorganizations, rumor, innuendo and the like. While every organizational environment will contain an inevitable amount of politics, socializing and undercurrent—all normal attributes of the human condition—they contain them to surprisingly different levels.

Ask yourself what's on most people's minds after a layoff is announced, or a downsizing effort is implemented. Most become consumed about their futures, their mortgages, the condition of their résumés, and how to keep a low profile during the reductions. Energy is diverted from the customer to self-survival. Yet this also occurs millions of times a day for lesser issues, such as the boss's perceived unfair treatment, poor working conditions, unresponsive colleagues, safety concerns, poor preparation, etc. The leader's responsibility is to minimize the distractions. Every arrow that the company launches should be directed at the bullseye, the customer. What are you doing to measure the total amount of available effort directed at the business goals of the organization?

It hardly matters how many sales calls the sales force completes. What matters is the amount of new business that's generated. The number of calls the service people answer each day is irrelevant compared to how many customers' concerns were effectively resolved (unresolved concerns simply generate additional phone calls, which can be answered and measured!). The amount of financial reports generated is unimportant, unless they can be pragmatically used to improve the business results next quarter.

Leaders too often attempt to "buy" their way out of problems by installing expensive quality programs, improvement processes and "programs *du jour*." These are actually *distractions*, often divorced from the need to please the customer and exceed business goals. They create internal bureaucracies, silos of new specialists who defend the approaches to the death, and a diversion of energy from the external to the internal.

Productivity improvement does not come from throwing people out the door. It comes most dramatically from moving internal focus to external focus, from measuring outputs

Ruthlessly Weed-Out Poor Managers

Suffer No Fools Gladly

When you observe poor performance in an operation, go immediately to the manager of that performer. If the performer isn't being either developed or removed, remove the manager..

THREE KEYS:

1. Management is not a circus. Provide no nets.
2. Every performance evaluation at every level should include developmental goals which are specific, keyed to a time frame, and are measurable.
3. Content knowledge does not inherently include process knowledge. An "expert" is not necessarily a good manager. Stop promoting the top sales person to sales manager simply on the basis of sales volume.

and not tasks, and from the minimization of internal disruption and internal disrupters.

There is no such phenomenon as a poor manager working in isolation. Every poor manager who is lousing up the operation is doing so through the kind offices of his or her superior. The buck never stops at incompetence. It stops where the authority to do something about the incompetence didn't act.

I explained once to a CEO that one of his direct reports was brutally treating people, verbally abusing them in public, and acting like a tyrant. "Well, that's Henry," said the CEO. "None of us approves of his behavior, but he does get results, and the rest of us would never use his techniques."

"I don't think you understand," said I, "that the employees believe that you *want* Henry to act that way, that you reward him for acting that way, and many of his subordinates are adapting his style. You are sanctioning his behavior by doing nothing. It is your style, not Henry's."

We have had an obsession with taking the easy route in promoting people. The best sales person became sales manager, the best photographer became photo editor, the best underwriter became underwriting manager, and so on and on and on. The problem with this lockstep process is that *content* expertise does not necessarily entail *process* expertise. Simply being good at a job does not qualify one to be good at managing others in that job, at developing people in the job, at accepting the accountabilities for the results of the job, for achieving collaborative relationships with other managers, etc. Some of us naturally possess "people skills." Most of us don't, and those skills are not automatically developed as we excel in our particular areas of expertise.

There are two commandments for leaders in choosing *other* leaders:

1. Carefully select, develop, mentor, evaluate and provide feedback to potential managers. This is the most important selection decision you make. Invest as much time in this as you would in your own development, if not more. Establish a process for evaluating candidates, using the criteria for the future job, not merely success in the former job. Remember that very few legendary athletic coaches and managers were star ball players themselves. The ability to develop and lead others is often divorced from performance in the jobs those others possess.

2. Ruthlessly weed-out incompetent managers. Suffer no fools gladly. The only worse decision than making a poor choice for a manager's position is to allow the poor choice to remain there. Bad managers ruin people, performance and values faster than competitors, poor economies or even the government ever could. A poor manager is a reflection on *your* beliefs and style. Develop that person or remove that person. Remember that poor people make poor choices, and inevitably surround themselves with poor people.

Many leaders make the mistake of providing too much safety for their key managers. By that I mean the leader is there with a safety net if the manager's decisions prove to be faulty. He or she will play the hero, and bail the subordinate out of difficulty. This is a disservice to all concerned. You must allow people to make mistakes, to fail, and to

Prevent Problems, Don't Solve Them

No One Ever Asks "Is There An Insurance Agent On Board?"

The problem solver has become the great American organizational hero. That's like erecting statues in honor of sprinkler systems and fire doors. The idea is *not to have to use them.*

THREE KEYS:

1. Focus on prevention, not correction. For every contingent action, put in place three preventive actions.
2. Celebrate the plans that proceed with a minimum of disruption. Make heroes out of the fire marshals, not just the fire fighters.
3. Equip people (and yourself) with fundamentally sound planning skills. If people's only skills are problem solving, guess what they'll wait to do?

learn from the experience. Your job is to help in the learning, not to avoid the fall. Unless there are consequences for our actions, we tend not to change our behavior.

If I always land in the net, the fall can be a pleasant ride.

We celebrate our fire fighters and police pursuits. Fair enough. Someone has to put out the fires and catch the criminals. But the real heroes are the fire marshals who ensure that dangerous conditions are eliminated, and cops on the beat whose presence prevents crime. Organizational "oil spills" are as difficult and expensive to clean up as was the Exxon Valdez. Think of the savings in preventing their occurrence.

We'll always need problem solvers, and they will always be in plentiful supply. It's the problem *preventers* who are a rare breed. It's one thing to have lower-level people concentrating on putting out fires. But what if our leaders are occupied with the same myopic view? Effective preventive actions will always save time, money, energy, focus and, yes, embarrassment. No one spends too much time praising the sprinkler system. They want to know who caused the fire...

ACTIONS

	present	future
cause	***corrective***	***preventive***
effect	***adaptive***	***contingent***

In the graph, we can see the only four actions available to us regarding problems, and they revolve around cause and effect, present and future. If a problem has already occurred, we can either ***correct*** it by removing its cause (patching the hole in the roof) or ***adapt*** to its effects (putting a bucket under the leak, or having people wear raincoats).

In the future, anticipating the problem, we can store buckets and raincoats in the closets as a ***contingency***, should the problem occur. But to ***prevent*** its occurrence, we build a roof with the most weather-resistant materials and with redundant layers of waterproofing. Do you think that airlines prefer to employ preventive actions or contingent actions? For that matter, how do you drive your car—attempting to avoid accidents through defensive driving, or aggressively and recklessly, knowing that you have insurance coverage?

Leaders who are heroic lead the charge into the latest problem and remove it, accepting the pain and loss as part of the job. And sometimes that is necessary, because nothing is assured in organizational life, and even the "unsinkable" Titanic would have been better served with more lifeboats. But leaders rush into that battle so often because they've spent too little time attempting to prevent its occurrence. Though not as glamorous and certainly "post-heroic" (or maybe "pre-heroic"!), it's the leader who's responsible for the planning, discipline and example of installing effective preventive actions.

Like all leadership disciplines, preventive action has a systematic approach:

Exploit Change, Don't Fear It

The Future Isn't What It Used to Be

The philosophy that "this, too, shall pass" has, ironically, become passé. Change is no longer accelerating. It's now constant.

THREE KEYS:

1. Create change. The best time to change something is when it's succeeding. Keep raising the bar.
2. Aggressively seek out the causes of your successes. Don't be overwhelmed finding out why you failed. We build on strengths, not on correcting weaknesses.
3. When a product, service or process is highly successful, don't seek to merely do more of it. Move laterally, attempting to connect other areas of the enterprise to the success.

Identify those potential problems that would have the greatest impact (typically safety, quality, image, etc.), identify what their likeliest causes would be (don't focus on effects, or you're already into contingencies), and describe and install the preventive actions which would most likely prevent the causes from developing.

Put the cop on the beat.

Change is a way of life as we turn the corner into a new century. This isn't just true of technology, where software is obsolete by the time it reaches the retail shelves. It's also true demographically, as the nature of the population changes; perceptually, as we continually question basic assumptions about health and moral choices; structurally, as we create leaner organizations and remove "boundaries"; and geopolitically, as even small businesses become entwined in the worldwide economy.

The leader's job isn't to react to it, but to *create* it. And, surprisingly perhaps, the best time to create it is when things are going well. You are always in the best condition to create change when acting from a position of strength. You are in the worst condition when acting from a position of desperation. When you're strong, you have the resources, momentum and confidence to take prudent risk. You also have the luxury of the "freedom to fail," because even total failure will not kill you.

The leader decides how high to raise the bar. Hewlett-Packard is probably the best example of an organization that is never content with the present height of the bar, even if it's the only one currently clearing it. HP continually "tears itself apart" striving to create outstanding organizations, processes, products and services where good ones already exist. It doesn't wait for someone else to clear the current height or, heaven forfend, to establish a new height. While the others are scurrying to catch up and remain in the competition, HP keeps raising the bar. That's what champions—and leaders—do.

The time to raise the bar is when you're already on top, or at least in good shape. We succeed most dramatically when building on our strengths, not by trying to correct weaknesses. (That's why problem solving must be subordinated to innovation and preventive actions.)

To raise the bar most effectively, we have to find why we're already good and exploit those characteristics in new ways. We are often swept away by trying to find out why we fail, why things went wrong, and what we can learn from those mistakes. That intent is sound, so long as it's not at the expense of also learning why we succeed. High sales, positive customer feedback and strong profits are wonderful, but they're not replecatable and not a means to raise the bar *unless we understand why* sales took off, why customers are so happy, and why costs are down.

Leaders take the initiative in setting new levels of performance, conditioning people to meet those new standards, and evaluating progress in reaching them. They demonstrate why it's important, how to achieve it, and then celebrate the success in

Ferociously Guard Your Time

"I Don't Have Time To Do That" Is An Oxymoron

We have time to do whatever we choose to do. "Choose" is the operative concept. Priorities should be of your own making, otherwise someone is stealing your time.

THREE KEYS:

1. Never allow anyone to delegate upward. No one can leave anything on your desk unless you give permission.
2. Constantly seek to eliminate tasks and duties which are low priority. Delegate them downward if needed. First try simply ignoring them for a few days. If no one yells, they're not needed.
3. Faithfully adopt the slogan, "No whining." Hang it on the wall. Point to it as needed.

reaching it—just prior to establishing another new height. Leaders create change. They set new goals. They make good organizations outstanding, and outstanding organizations superb.

Any organization which is on a plateau is in that position because it has leaders who can no longer climb.

Time is of the essence. Haste makes waste. A stitch in time saves nine. Time waits for no man. The time is now. We have all the time in the world. It seems as though we're always getting conflicting messages about time. In fact, if we read all the books extant on time management, we'd have no time to do anything else!

Leaders must rigorously guard their time. The phrase "I have no time for that" is oxymoronic. Of course you have the time, but you simply don't choose to spend it on that issue. Unfortunately, that issue is sometimes a child's athletic game, a local fund-raiser, a family event, self-development and attention to one's spouse.

I'm constantly hearing executives bemoan the fact that they don't know where their time goes. Well, I know where it goes. It's being stolen. Keep hold of your time as tightly as you do your wallet.

Leaders invest their time in the most important priorities facing the organization: exemplifying values, developing people, understanding the customer, setting and implementing strategy, celebrating victories. They also have the time available for the legitimate crisis and unanticipated problem. They can do so because they *are not* in wall-to-wall meetings and conferences. Every leader should have *discretionary, unplanned* time available every day of every week. Leaders are judged by their results, not their actions. Keeping constantly busy simply indicates that you're rowing the boat instead of setting its course.

Here are the primary defenses against time thieves:

- Never make decisions which can be made at lower levels or which have already been made at lower levels, unless you find an absolutely fatal flaw.
- Do not wordsmith or rewrite other people's memos. If people don't understand, they'll let the writer know.
- Life isn't about perfection. Merely because you can do something better does not justify your doing it. In most cases, 98% is better than 102% for ROI.
- Handle items once. If you keep looking at the same piece of paper, decide to a) take action immediately, b) delegate it, c) throw it out. No other options.
- Attend as few meetings as possible. Never attend simply because your title is desired there, or people are afraid of not having you present. Attend only when there's an issue demanding your participation. Meetings are the *absolute worst* vehicles to use solely for the exchange of information.
- Answer your own phone and make your own calls. If you don't want to speak to the caller, say so.
- Put reading and reference material in one place, and go through it at the end of the day. Either read it, file it, or dispose of it at that time.
- Inform people that if you have to play the referee on issues, you're going to do so rapidly and according only to your interests. Explain that both parties might be far better off with a compromise that they construct themselves.
- Never let anyone leave anything on your desk without your permission. Never give permission to anyone other than your secretary, and watch him or her like a hawk.

Don't Sweat the Small Stuff

De minimis non curat praetor.

Leaders watch the big picture. They view the world through a telescope, not a microscope. Details are important, but that's why you have employees.

THREE KEYS:

1. Delegate details and follow-up. The content should be handled by managers and supervisors, the process by secretaries and administrative assistants.
2. Approve plans and outcomes. Have others develop and review the steps and the input. That's what lawyers, accountants and consultants are for.
3. Never do failure work. If you're doing something because someone else failed to, or you didn't do it right to begin with, you're killing the organization.

• Schedule weekly time for recreation, leisure, hobbies, self-development, family, community and/or just plain fun. You have to recharge your batteries if they're to be at peak performance on the job.

Remember: You have the time to do anything you choose to do.

When Ford first purchased Jaguar, Ford officials (who were never exactly cast as the avatars of automotive quality themselves) visiting the British plant were aghast to find teams of workers whose sole job it was to fix the defects coming off the assembly line. Quality wasn't built-in, it was addended after-the-fact!

The people who should have been "sweating" those details were the employees. But management decided on a system which obviated the need to watch the details (i.e., do careful, precise work) and actually encouraged sloppiness. In fact, when a Jaguar worker's quota of engines or doors or windshields was completed for the day, the worker could stop working, even it were only mid-day! Without a quality standard, I'll work as fast as I can for as little time as possible, too!

Leaders look at the big picture, make decisions based upon strategic business goals and long-term objectives, and provide guidance for subordinates in working toward those ends. But they allow others *to do* the work, applying judgment and discretion to the "how" of the steps.

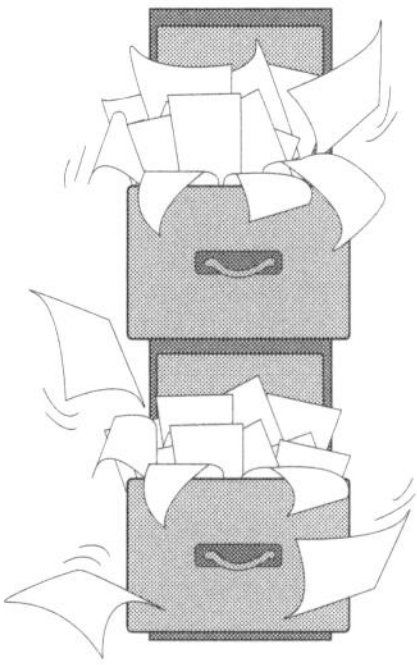

Look around you. How many of your peers are spending time reviewing and rewriting someone else's memo, altering the steps in someone else's plan, deciding on issues which could be done (usually better) at much lower level, and occupying themselves with small operational details? It has been reliably reported that Jimmy Carter, when President, was so enmeshed in detail that he even decided on the scheduling for the White House tennis courts. Do you recall how he looked after four years in office? He had aged by 20 years. Nor was his detail fixation rewarded with the public's esteem at the next election.

Carter's behaviors were more than idiosyncratic. They deprived him of valuable time that could have been spent on a defining vision for his administration, on affairs of state, and, not incidentally, on his own relaxation and reinvigoration.

High energy levels are wonderful *if* they are directed at the issues for which you are evaluated, and you are undoubtedly *not* evaluated on details. In many cases I've observed leaders performing tasks that could easily be done by their secretaries.

Use these strategies to clean off your desk, clean out your mental files, and remain focused on the distant future rather than the minuscule present:

- Trust your subordinates, and capitalize on that trust by delegating virtually all details and follow-up to them.
- If that trust isn't present, ask yourself if it's unfamiliarity with their work, an unsubstantiated bias on your part, or evidence of their incompetence.
- Take steps to familiarize yourself with subordinates, overcome biases and perceptions by focusing on evidence, and developing or replacing those who do not have sufficient competence to accept the delegation.

Then sit back, put your feet up, and *think* about what your area of responsibility is to accomplish. You are paid for results, not arbitrary actions. How much time are

Direct reports will try to "protect" you from information they feel does not warrant your attention. Like *The New York Times*, it's "all the news ***(we see)*** fit to print."

THREE KEYS:

1. Create and maintain "pulse points" throughout the organization.
2. Make sure you have independent access to, and communication from, customers.
3. Provide clear behavioral indicators that encourage, not discourage, subordinates to approach you with all information that merits your attention.

you allowing yourself to accomplish them?

The ancient Romans used the phrase which is the title of this segment. It translates as, "The magistrate does not consider trifles." Neither should you.

A human resources vice president at a major health care center prided himself on "protecting" his boss, the CEO. "I manage the president," he would explain, not so much as a boast as a fundamental fact of conducting his job. "I'll determine what's presented to him, because he needs to be protected from the random and uncontrolled feedback from the employees. I have his ear."

Unfortunately for the human resources guy, I had the other ear, and he was on his way to manage some other boss at another organization within the year.

Human behavior is such that people feel an irresistible force compelling them to tell the boss exactly what they perceive the boss wants to hear. Before we inveigh against these dastardly people and cowardly practices, ask yourself this: How accommodating are you when people approach you with "bad" news? Do you jump up and down, raise your voice, immediately try to find out whose "fault" it is, curse the fates, and/or rhetorically question why you have to do everything yourself to get it done right? If any of this is applicable, I might not want to disturb your complacency, either.

You must provide clear behavioral indicators that you *need*—not will reluctantly entertain—to hear bad news as well as good news. You must reward the behaviors which reinforce subordinates' willingness to approach you with setbacks, problems, obstacles and outright defeat. Subordinates have to understand that you believe their greatest contribution is to tell the whole truth, not to shield you from unwelcome truths.

Irrespective of your success in encouraging candid feedback, you must develop alternative "pulse points" in the organization and among customers. This doesn't mean undermining staff and frightening the local populace. It does mean the "managing by wandering around" that most people love to quote but haven't a clue as to what it entails. Observe the operation. Ask yourself if it reflects the reality that is created in the dialogue you have at meetings and with subordinates. If you've been told that people are putting in ten-hour days and staff is lean, yet you observe long, leisurely chats among people and plenty of time at the coffee machine, then you have a splendid case of cognitive dissonance. If you're told that morale is high, yet you hear complaints, observe short fuses and learn of customer attrition, there's probably more to the story.

How are you arranging to validate the reality that's created for you by your daily sources of input? What are you doing to independently validate that the image being perpetrated of the company is the same one that the customers perceive?

It's not enough to be looking far ahead, trying to survey the landscape. You have to make sure that, while doing so, you're not peering into a mirror or an optical illu-

Articulate and Demonstrate Clear Ethical Positions

Either Stand Like A Rock Or Swim With the Current

Leaders should not hesitate to exhibit healthy outrage. On important issues, let others know exactly where you stand. It's better to be wrong in a good cause than equivocate on tough issues.

THREE KEYS:

1. Determine which issues are worth dying for, and put your back against the wall if they arise. If they arise daily, you're probably fighting for taste, not principle, and you will die.
2. Where matters of taste are concerned, go with the flow. No one has a monopoly on good taste, but it's these conflicts which are often the most costly.
3. Never compromise on a basic belief or value. Agreeing to a small bribe is like agreeing to be a little dead. Some things *are* clear and unequivocal

sion. Nor do you need "protection" from your employees and customers. Are there figurative "toughs" surrounding you, or CIA-types with earphones and dark glasses?

Send home the clowns. Your ears are your own.

No less a scholar and patriot than Thomas Jefferson said, "In matters of principle, stand like a rock; in matters of taste, swim with the tide." Leaders must show a combination of healthy outrage and rigorous reaction to threats to basic values and beliefs, and a tolerance and accommodation for varied styles and approaches. Are you clear about what will prompt you to stand, and what will encourage you to swim?

I've seen people "go to the mat" over who has access to equipment, whose division will get new furniture first, and whose vacation policies should prevail. I've also seen people "look the other way" when vendors offer kickbacks, expense accounts are obviously padded, and sales are reported this year that really won't be delivered until next year. As a controller at GE said during one of our ethics workshops, "In for a dime, in for a dollar. There's no such thing as minor cheating with the company's money. It's all unethical, the amounts notwithstanding."

Leaders are able to choose the issues which represent their basic belief systems and the core values of the organization, and are unafraid to stand alone in a crowd to defend them against short-term exigencies. One of the most common assaults is the claim, ironically, of multiculturalism, used in a perverted manner: "Bribes are common in other cultures," we're told (usually by someone having trouble making a sale or seriously behind plan) "and we're at a disadvantage by pretending we're too good to offer them." It's one thing to be part of a team rejecting such nonsense, but it's another to be odd-person-out when colleagues are facing a lean year-end. Leaders don't equivocate about basic values. They take strong stands and damn the torpedoes. Farragut stormed into Mobile Bay because the need to win that battle—and, hence, the war—was far greater than the potential loss of a few of his ships. Full speed ahead...

If people perceive that it's all right to bend the rules, the rules won't be swayed, they'll be destroyed. You can't be a little pregnant and you can't be an occasional cheat. You are or you aren't. Leaders have to be willing not only to reprimand or terminate subordinate transgressions, but also to respond to peer and superior transgressions. No one can lead others when they are visibly cowed and intimidated. Among the worst of these cases I've seen is when inappropriate language and/or humor is stated in public, and colleagues believe they're on high moral ground because they don't join in the language or the laughter. In fact, *passivity sanctions behavior*. If you're not against it, then you're for it.

Leadership requires taking positions and taking stands over what matters. It also requires "going along" when the issues are not threatening basic beliefs. The latter includes presentation style, attire, and frames of reference, to name just a few. The leader who allows a sexist remark but objects to slides which don't adhere to a cer-

On-the-job training is to learning as trial-and-error is to problem solving. It will eventually produce results, but at huge cost in effectiveness and efficiency.

THREE KEYS:

1. Actively mentor a diverse group of people, not solely those who look like you or share your background.
2. Do not provide special favors, but rather special challenges. Mentoring is not about short-cuts and corner-cutting, it's about accountability and growth.
3. Focus overwhelmingly on strong performers who can provide spectacular contributions. Mentoring is not remedial work.

tain format has the organizational universe upside-down.

Put your back against the wall and defend the values you and the organization hold dear. You may occasionally get bloody, but you'll seldom be killed. And if you are, you'll undoubtedly be leaving for a better place.

We've heard a lot about the "learning organization.[1] However, people in organizations don't just learn unless someone is educating. There are alternatives, of course: self-study books, video tapes, motivational cassettes, external and internal trainers, on-the-job experience, operations manuals, and so forth. However, these alternatives are merely adjuncts to the real organizational educator: The leader who provides both formal and informal direction on a personal, one-on-one basis.

In our client surveys, we've learned that the factor most consistently reported as being responsible for promotion and career success—above job assignment, educational background, luck and even performance evaluations—is mentoring. I'm not referring so much to the "champion," who aggressively pushes his or her candidate for the next promotion or plum assignment. I'm referring to the true mentor who provides confidential and personalized help in one's learning, feedback on performance, and a sounding board for difficulties and problems.

Moving successfully within organizations is not unlike playing a game of chess. Different pieces have different capabilities. Strategy must guide tactics. Sometimes trade-offs and sacrifices make sense. At times the board is clear and decipherable, at other times the disposition of the pieces is hard to interpret and the future is cloudy. And there is a point when the lowliest of pieces can become the most powerful of pieces.

Leaders mentor others. They mentor others who are not necessarily like themselves in terms of gender, race, ethnicity, points of view, frames of reference, education, background, dress, native language and other distinctions. By doing so, leaders not only provide personal growth for diverse people, but they send the message that doing so is important (see the first chapter, Speak Through Your Actions). Ideally, they mentor others who may not be in their own departments or their own division, as well as those who are.

Perhaps most importantly, leaders invest most of their time in the top performers, not in remedial work with poor performers. Every organization achieves the most dramatic success by leveraging its most talented people, not by tweaking its marginal performers. The organization's performance system should be invoked to help poor performers improve, or to replace them. This may seem harsh, but it's one of the greatest failures of leadership. To use a baseball analogy: A team is far more enhanced by helping its .320 hitters to become .333 hitters than it is by helping its .220 hitters become .245 hitters. Don't ignore poor performance; put systems in place to provide remediation. But do focus on strong performance, or at least strong *potential.*

Mentoring isn't for life. Find some new people each year as those from the past need less access to you. At the end of each year you should be able to point to a handful of talented, high-potential people who have learned, grown and improved their contributions to the organization in some part due to your personal involvement in their education.

Never Play for the Tie

Celebrate Victories, Learn from Defeats

Remember "benign neglect"? No one's blood was ever stirred by a leader who stood in front of the troops and said, "Let's dare to be conservative!" Strive for nothing less than victory, settle for nothing less than excellence

THREE KEYS:

1. Establish bold goals and exciting objectives. "No pain, no gain."
2. Eschew "playing it safe" and trying to manipulate the plans. Otherwise you're telling people that the bookkeeping is more important than the performance.
3. Compete with all guns blazing and all talents employed. Organizations are in competition and, given a choice, it's better to win than to lose. I can guarantee that the shareholders feel that way. So do your customers.

Leaders teach. When they do, people learn and organizations profit.

[1]First popularized by the *The Fifth Discipline: The Art & Practice of the Learning Organization*, by Peter M. Senge, Doubleday: 1990.

Many years ago, Notre Dame was playing its final football game of the season against Michigan State. If Notre Dame won, they would be undisputed national champions (a "mythical" and unofficial title) in all of the polls. Michigan, however, played a superb game. With two minutes left in the contest, the score was tied and Notre Dame gained possession of the ball in its own end of the field.

At that point, one of my great epiphanies took place, right in the living room in front of the television. Because what transpired was truly astounding. Tens of thousands of people in the stands and millions like me prepared for a frantic Notre Dame drive to the Michigan goal. Instead, we saw Notre Dame *run out the clock* by running a series of uninspired plays into the Michigan line. Michigan fans and players booed. Notre Dame fans booed. I booed.

We found out later that the Notre Dame coach, Ara Parsighian, had determined—accurately—that a tie would also guarantee his team the national title. So rather than play for a win, with its attendant risks of a fumble or interception, the coach decided to play for a tie to attain a theoretical national championship. It was the most visible, magnificent and egregious example of poor leadership I had ever witnessed in all of sports. Here we had a great example for our youth—play it safe, forget the spirit of the contest, ignore the tradition of this great institution, and help the leader gain repute for his career. Unfortunately, we see examples of Notre Dame's tie in organizations every day.

A woman who once worked for me had a sign on her desk which said, "You win some, you lose some, and some get rained-out. But you have to suit-up for them all." As long as we're getting dressed for the game, why don't we also try to win it?

Set dramatic targets for your operation, then provide the means to help people achieve them. Organizations compete. This is not a repugnant phrase nor an immoral act. It's the basis of our free enterprise system. Enter the fray with all guns firing, all hands on deck, and everyone focused on the target. No one enters the Olympics shouting "Go for the bronze!" Pursuing the gold and ending up with the bronze is a noble effort, but pursuing the bronze and ending up in 12th place makes little sense.

Celebrate those victories. They are nothing to be ashamed of, and too often they are taken for granted. In essence, this says to people, "You succeeded, but not by enough." When tough goals are achieved, take time to lead the celebration, literally and figuratively. Provide people with a momento. Buy them lunch. Put their pictures in the paper. Ask their families to participate. Allow them to enjoy success.

Conversely, when you haven't been successful, learn from the setback and refocus your efforts. Don't immediately cut back and pull in your horns. Can you imagine an athletic club, after a mediocre season, announcing to the season ticket holders that it has decided to *cut back* on the training room hours, the number of conditioning coaches, the quality of the equipment and the number of quality players? Yet that's exactly what poor leadership does after a setback.

Remember Notre Dame. Never play for the tie. Success is never final and failure

Lead Your Community

People Should Follow Your Guidance, Not Fear Your Power

The true test of a leader is whether others recognize the attributes of leadership when the "LEADER" sign is not in evidence. In other words, do those outside the organizational property lines follow as enthusiastically as those who are afraid not to?

THREE KEYS:

1. Volunteer in the community, in charitable organizations, in political groups and in social settings. Leaders are who they are because of their energy, their attributes, their initiative, and not because they have a corner office or lengthy title.
2. Leadership under varied conditions improves the ability to lead under all conditions. Deliberately place yourself in unfamiliar circumstances.
3. Observe the leadership traits of those in other settings. What are they doing which you can adopt, and what are they doing which you should avoid?

If leadership is about helping others to improve, leveraging one's talents and contributions through others, and achieving results for the organization, then leaders must acquire a certain amount of power—clout— if they are to be successful. That power can originate in a variety of sources, some of which are much more effective than others.

There are five primary origins of power, although I'm sure you can amend and modify the list, depending upon how detailed you wish to be. But for our purposes here, these are the fundamental sources:

1. Reward: The ability to provide both tangible and intangible gratification to the performers. If people recognize that you can bestow salary increases, public recognition, learning and development, desirable assignments and/or simply credible "pats on the back," you will derive power from that recognition.

2. Punishment: Conversely, the wherewithal to create consequences, ranging from chastisement to financial pain—and even loss of livelihood—is a strong factor in possessing power.

3. Authority: The clear acceptance that, by dint of your position and title, you are capable of actions that affect others' performance is another source of power. In other words, you have the unquestioned right to approve my expenses, assign my territory or withhold resources. Usually, title bestows authority.

4. Expertise: Your knowledge and experience—your wisdom—create an environment in which people are willing to allow you to take the lead. Your ability to provide information, analyze situations, suggest solutions and define issues places you in a leadership relationship.

5. Referent: This is the charisma test. Your charm, likeability, suave nature and other attributes afford you the default position of leadership when people gather together. Others willingly subordinate themselves to your personality.

Note that these are not mutually-exclusive, nor are they all position-dependent. *The best leaders are those whom people enthusiastically want to follow, not those who demand fealty, loyalty or conformity.* The best test for leaders is outside of their organizational turf. What are you doing in the community—for civic associations, charities, public events, professional organizations, fund-raising—to provide your talents and leadership skills?

Commensurately, you will learn how to lead those who don't have to follow you unless they choose to: colleagues, volunteers, members, association executives, etc. *Pro bono* work can have a huge payback for you as you hone your leadership behaviors.

What is your level of commitment and involvement in activities outside of work? If you belong to associations and volunteer groups, are you content to be a member, or do you strive for leadership? Or, ideally, do you seem to gravitate toward leadership as others vest you with their respect and support?

Leaders don't remove the mantle when they remove their business attire. Respect doesn't stop at the company property line.

Influence Others Through Enlightened Self-Interest

Help Others to Motivate Themselves

True motivation is intrinsic. It stems from the individual discovering various means to meet his or her self-interset, which is different from self-serving or selfish. It is, therefore, self-perpetuating. You don't need a big stick to get attention. But you do need to pay attention if it's going to stick.

THREE KEYS:

1. Do not use raw power—threat, fear and intimidation—in an attempt to establish motivation. You will get only movement, and only as long as you have the heaviest weapons.
2. Be very leery of peer pressure as a motivating force. It is notoriously fickle, lasts an indeterminate length of time, and may actually turn out to be counter to the organization's best interests.
3. Do not work at "motivating" an employee. Instead, work to establish an environment which is conducive to all employees motivating themselves. The former is hard work. The latter is inspired leadership.

Motivation is one of my favorite topics with leaders. Some claim that fear is sufficient. Others are confident that the sole motivator worth consideration is financial. There are those who feel that whatever motivates them should motivate their followers. "Throwing open your briefcase in front of a roaring fire and working all night!" shouted one of my former bosses, when I asked what motivated him. It's a safe bet that he wasn't in a whole lot of company in our company. Bill Gates, CEO of Microsoft and wealthiest man in this cosmos, says simply, "Put the best people in a room, get out of their way, and throw in some fresh meat every so often."

There are three basic forms of behavior change available to leaders:

1. Power: Hold a figurative "gun" to someone's head and ask if they wouldn't mind doing something for you. This gets immediate attention, but seldom has an effect after the gun is withdrawn (which often prompts a counter-action). Voltaire said that "God is on the side of the heaviest battalions." Perhaps, but motivation is not.

2. Peer Pressure: The psychologists call this "normative" pressure. Don't be the only one who isn't with the "in" crowd. My superiors at Prudential Insurance used to inform me that I would be the only manager at my level who did not make the maximum contribution to the United Way campaign. Later, of course, I found out they told everyone the exact same thing before anyone had donated. Peer pressure is fickle, tough to control, and can run counter to organizational goals.

3. Rational self-interest. Help me to understand how my own goals will be met (tangible and intangible, ego-centered and externally-centered, short-term and long-term) and allow me to vigorously and enthusiastically pursue the goal. (See chapter 3 on aligning organizational and individual goals.)

Motivation is about commitment, not compliance. The varied and diverse people in your organization have varied and diverse interests and needs. "Blanket" motivational programs virtually never encompass that diversity, and "competitions" foster winners and losers.

Enlightened leaders provide environments in which all people can identify their own self-interest as compatible with the organization's goals. But those cultures don't magically appear. They must be carefully nurtured by the leader, and the qualities and attributes of that environment must be modeled and exemplified by leadership.

Those environments feature:

- open and two-way communication
- timely feedback
- constructive critique
- immediate consequences (rewards and punishments)
- subordination of ego
- the freedom to fail
- continual learning and growth
- support and protection for innovators

Movement is about the dogged pursuit of goals under duress. Motivation is about exceeding goals as a constructive human condition. Leaders settle for nothing less.

Identify Your Heroes

Take Me to Your Leader

Learn why you have followed those you've most respected. What were the traits that attracted and motivated you? Why was it those people, in those conditions, at those times? The answers will provide insight into the leadership that others require of you.

THREE KEYS:

1. You can't be an effective leader unless you've been an effective follower. Determine what has prompted you to follow the lead of others.
2. Leadership is not a single entity which can be studied, which is why there are 19 chapters in this booklet. Evaluate yourself in terms of skills, behaviors and attributes.
3. Determine what the leadership demands will be tomorrow, and focus on them today. It does no good to be mastering the art of leading a cavalry charge in the 21st Century

I once shared a stage with a speaker who was apoplectic about the need for having heroes. Our audience was composed of 100 high-achieving high school sophomores, who listened with rapt attention. He challenged them to name their heroes, and combatively demanded why they chose the ones they did.

Inevitably, during the question and answer session, a student asked my colleague who his heroes were. He stammered and sweated for almost 60 seconds, and then half-heartedly blurted out, “Well, I’d have to say my high school teachers,” as he desperately sought out the teachers in the room for support. They gave him not an ounce of it, because they had seen he was a fraud. He preached a position he did not practice. He was no leader. He was a con man.

What has caused you to follow others in terms of personal attributes, conditions, timing or personal fulfillment? Are there likely to be similar conditions and similar needs among those you are to lead? What have you learned from your heroes? How have your heroes changed as you’ve matured, traveled, learned and changed? What are the conditions that will demand leadership tomorrow, and how are you preparing yourself today to meet them? Finally, what are your feedback sources to help you evaluate your progress? To this day I have a vivid memory of former New York City Mayor Ed Koch standing amidst hustling morning commuters, repeatedly asking, “How am I doing? How am I doing?”

Give yourself a score in the categories below. None of us is perfect. Where do you have to improve? *In what areas do you need information, because you’re not sure about your performance or capabilities?*

Skills	**R**[2]	**Behaviors**	**R**	**Other Attributes**	**R**
• Decision Making		• Assertiveness		• Experience in a Job	
• Problem Solving		• Persuasiveness		• Communications	
• Innovation		• Empowering Others		• Careful Listening	
• Strategy & Planning		• Flexibility		• Encouraging Others	
• Time Management		• High Energy		• Resolving Conflict	
• Setting Priorities		• Prudent Risk Taking		• Developing Others	

There are, obviously, more items to enter on these lists. Create your own, focusing on the unique needs of your particular leadership accountabilities, your constituency, and your organization. Add the attributes of your heroes, no matter who they may be.

On my office wall is a picture of Sandy Koufax, the great Dodger pitcher who was probably one of the very best in the history of organized baseball. Whenever he pitched, he sought perfection. And when he was in his best form, he was virtually unhittable, winning games for a punchless offense by 1-0 and 2-1 scores consistently over the years. His talent, artistry, focus and pursuit of excellence led his team to championships, and helped others to perform at levels which exceeded their own talents. He retired while at the very top of his form. My hero.

---

[2]Rate yourself in any manner comfortable, i.e., 10-1 or high-low. The point is to arrive at a *relative* assessment of your strengths and developmental needs among theses few examples. The three columns are independent—don’t associate them laterally

Raise the Bar

Steer the Vehicle, Unless You're Just Along for the Ride

I've never yet seen anyone race into the office screaming "Let's maintain the current level of performance!" I have, however, seen leaders who assume they've done their job by building fortresses on a plateau.

THREE KEYS:

1. Innovate whenever possible, restore only when absolutely necessary.
2. Reward risk takers and those who are unafraid to depart from the safe and secure.
3. Remind yourself and your people about just how stupid you all were two years ago. As you gain knowledge and experiences, you should also be gaining new alternatives to better achieve goals.

In the book *Masada*, Roman General Flavious Silva is congratulated on his great victory by one of his subordinates. Silva turns on the man and shouts, "Victory? We have won a rock in the middle of a wasteland on the shore of a poisoned sea!" As a leader, Silva could celebrate victories as well as anyone, but he also knew when the victory was hollow or pyrrhic. He had his own standards for success which were not reduced or demeaned by others who would settle for less.

The nature of your accomplishments will depend upon the height at which you set the bar. In pole vault and high jump competition, the last person in the match, even though already the victor through elimination, continues to jump at higher levels until they are eliminated at that new height. At top competitive levels, that height is always a national or world record. At lower level competitions, that height might be the meet, state or scholastic record. Nonetheless, the competition doesn't end *until the final competitor is through competing against his or her own personal best.*

Leaders raise the bar on a continual basis, even if they are already the world record holders. The best organizations I've ever observed—Hewlett-Packard, Merck & Co., Levi-Strauss—continually seek to improve on their best efforts. They literally tear themselves apart at times, in order to seek out still better ways of meeting business goals. Sometimes, in so doing, the bar gets knocked to the ground. No matter. They replace it at the new height and keep attempting to negotiate it.

To "lead" means to show the way; to guide; to precede. It's impossible to fulfill that mission by standing still and admiring the surroundings. Every day that you've visited the office and left again during which nothing new has happened, no goals have been furthered, no innovation has transpired and no new approaches have been entertained, is a day without leadership. Extend that to a week or a month or a year, and leadership vacuums develop. If the organization is, nevertheless, moving forward and on to new heights, it's certainly not due to any leadership on your part.

Managing the status quo and administering current affairs are for the managers and administrators. Leadership isn't needed to rally people around the mundane and every-day. Leadership is needed to rally people from an unexpected downturn and/or to propel them toward a desired future.

Are you simply "doing your job" every day, or are you helping others to do theirs still better? Are you watching as your operation achieves its usual standards of performance, or are you raising the standards? Are you reacting to problems, trying to fix and restore norms, or are you innovating and creating new and higher norms to which people can aspire? Are you satisfying your customers, or delighting them? Do you have compliant employees or committed employees? Are you content to be a reflection of your business, industry and society, or are you consumed with setting the standards for your business, industry and society?

Unless your answer is an unequivocal "The latter!" to each of those choices, then you're not guiding, you're simply along for the ride. Flavious Silva would not approve.

Do Not Walk in the Footsteps of Great People

Seek What They Sought

Leaders should be absolutely consistent about values but flexible about style. The search for a "perfect style" is illusory. Conditions and people change much too often.

THREE KEYS:

1. There are no perfect leadership styles. Try to be as flexible as possible while remaining aware of your options.
2. No matter what the circumstances or the styles involved, ensure that you are unqualifyingly consistent about the values and beliefs you represent. Compromise on the "how," never the "what."
3. Retain your perspective at all times. The world will not come to an end tomorrow, hard as it may be to believe, because of your decisions today.

The Starship Enterprise had a mission to "seek out new worlds." There was little precedent for what it was doing, so its captains often created alternatives and responses as they went along. However, the goals were clear, the ethical boundaries were in place, and each captain's "message" was absolutely consistent over time.

Over three hundred years ago, philosopher Matsuo Basho said, "Do not seek to follow in the footsteps of the men of old; seek what they sought." His advice should be a mandate for all leaders today.

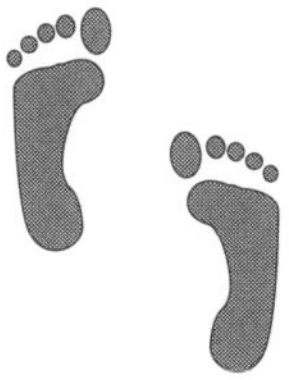

There are no "perfect" leadership styles. In fact, the pursuit of them has resulted in a plethora of labels assigned to people which do more to categorize and explain them away rather than aid in our understanding of them. Are you an INTJ, or "high D," or "expressive analytic," or a left-brainer, or perhaps a 9,1 on the grid, or a third quadrant, or an early adapter, or a pragmatist, or something of an intuitor? And how about your people? Do they need autonomy, coaching, empathy, independence, power, facts, pictures, tasks, or vanilla ice cream, while rappelling down a mountain?

Our research has overwhelmingly demonstrated that there are multiple styles available to the leader, based upon:

- the leader's own predispositions and preferences
- the environment
- the urgency
- the styles of the others who are involved
- the need for subordinate development
- the importance of the issue
- the degree to which commitment is required
- the range of alternatives available
- the degree of ownership sought
- the degree to which information is available

Don't concern yourself with style, but with results. Don't do what others have done in similar circumstances before you, pursue the proper goals. Understand that varied conditions and circumstances may well call for differing styles from the same leader. However, never compromise on the values. The "how" is flexible; the "what" seldom is.

There are no perfect leaders, just people who are trying, every day, to set an example for others, to guide them in pursuit of excellence, and to take the risks incumbent in modern-day decision making. Leaders dare to do things differently. They abhor the status quo. They don't copy others, but they do learn from others' successes and attributes. They don't demand that others copy them, but do help others learn from their experiences through mentoring and accessibility.

Leaders are concerned about substance, not style, steak and not sizzle. They seek knowledge and provide wisdom. And they know that tomorrow is always a new day, bringing with it fresh challenges and the opportunity to try new approaches.

Perhaps the final test of leaders is that every day others can see them, suited-up for the contest, and riding forward.

Select Your Own Three Keys Right Now

You can't lead others merely with good intentions. Decide what you will do, how you will do it, and when you will start. Remember, you only need 1% a day to be twice as good a leader within 70 days!

THREE KEYS:

1. ________________________________

2. ________________________________

3. ________________________________

There is nothing about leadership which relies upon the muse, the stroke of lightening or the mystical and magical. Nothing in the prior pages suggests alchemy or eye of newt. Our research reveals that leaders successfully raise the standards every day when they develop and possess the volition, skills, behaviors and attributes to do so. It's as simple as that.

This booklet has tried to provide some of those skills and techniques, which are relatively easy to master and implement. You lead by example. You exemplify values. You take (and reward) prudent risk. Setting higher standards and higher levels of expectation is not a gamble. In fact, refusing or ignoring the need to create new levels of performance is the largest risk facing most organizations. It's not a dearth of resources which causes enterprises to stagnate, it's a dearth of leadership. And as we've tried to illustrate, leadership can be anywhere in the organization, at any level, dealing with any issue. It's not hierarchical. It's referent.

Leading is not heroic, but post-heroic. It's about helping others to achieve their greatest possible potential, thereby enabling the organization to achieve the most dramatic possible business goals. In our experience, leaders are made, not born.

While some people may accept the mantle more easily than others, and possess more native skills for the role, all of us can learn to be better at leadership. It does not come naturally by dint of promotion. It comes with hard work, concern for others, and by dint of emotion.

No one in your organization believes what they read, what they hear, or even what you tell them. They only believe what they see. What are you doing as an exemplar to demonstrate the organization's values, your vision of the future, and the height of the bar? What are the advertent and inadvertent messages you are sending? When they look at you, are they seeing a bold leader setting the pace, or a timid soul defending the current position?

If your view of your organization—large or small, public or private, product or service—is one that encompasses a group of talented people whose abilities are vital to the success of the enterprise, then everything in this booklet should make pragmatic business sense. It's up to you to determine what you will take from these chapters and guidelines which will enable you to exploit those abilities and ensure they are applied in the continual effort to move forward, to achieve, to excel.

You can work hard by managing and administering, or you can work smart by leading others and leveraging their talents. The choice is yours.

Thus far you've been a passive participant in the processes described on these pages. Now it's time for you to be innovative and proactive. What will you do—now, immediately—to implement the ideas which can help your operation? The final three keys are yours. Every minute that you delay you are losing money, less able to enjoy success and, most importantly, less able to leverage your own talents to help others.

What are you going to do about it? Choose any of the ideas and approaches in this booklet, modify them for your business environment, and list specifically what you will begin to do in the box on the opposite page.

Now do it!

There are additional resources to help you listed on the following pages.

Additional Resources for Professionals from Alan Weiss

Books

Million Dollar Consulting: The Professional's Guide to Growing A Practice
McGraw-Hill: 1992, 1994, 1997 (292 pages, hard cover)

The definitive work on dramatically growing a consulting business. For the single practitioner, small firm principal, or aspiring consultant. The section on fee-setting alone is worth the price of the book. Main selection of the Fortune and Business Week Book Clubs. "If you're interested in becoming a rich consultant, this book is a must read." —Robert F. Mager, Founder and President, Mager Associates, member, Training & Development Hall of Fame.

Best Laid Plans: Turning Strategy Into Action Throughout Your Organization
HarperCollins: 1990; Las Brisas Research Press: 1994 (254 pages, hard cover)

How to implement strategy for any size organization, public or private, based upon the author's actual strategy work. Most strategy does not fail in its formulation, it fails in its implementation. This book addresses that failing. "I would have helped The New York Times company more if I had read it ten years ago."—Jack Harrison, Pulitzer Prize-winning Group President.

Managing for Peak Performance: A Guide to the Power (and Pitfalls) of Personal Style
HarperCollins: 1989; Las Brisas Research Press: 1994 (177 pages, hard cover)

Techniques for understanding and influencing others, including self-tests, instruments, guidelines and checklists for assessing style. Translated into German. Useful for stress reduction, selection, decision making and negotiating. "A uniquely practical set of guidelines for managing to get the results you need."—P. Roy Vagelos, Chairman and CEO, Merck & Co., Inc.

The Innovation Formula: How Organizations Turn Change Into Opportunity
(with Michel Robert) HarperCollins: 1988, 1990 (126 pages, soft cover)

The classic book on the process of innovation, for the individual as well as the organization. Translated into German and Italian. Provides tangible, measurable means to identify, evaluate and implement innovative ideas, including the assessment of risk. "A rational, sensible approach to making innovation a repeatable process."—Robert D. Kennedy, CEO, Union Carbide.

Cassettes

The Consultant's Treasury

Las Brisas Research Press: 1996 (two workbooks, four tapes, running time; 4 hours)

Three live speeches and one radio interview on marketing, visibility, credibility, value-based fees, proposals, and related topics for the professional consultant and/or speaker. Two workbooks contain questions and approaches to use with prospects as well as actual sample proposals. A must for every solo practitioner, new or veteran.

Ordering information on page 51.

Additional Resources for Professionals from Alan Weiss

Booklets: The Professional Development Series from Las Brisas Research Press

How to Maximize Fees in Professional Service Firms: A Handbook for Professionals

The methods for creating high-value client relationships and receiving commensurate fees for that value. Provides a provocative set of questions, keys and approaches which any professional can apply to his or her practice, irrespective of the field. Useful for the individual practitioner, small business owner, or individual member of any professional services firm.

Rejoicing in Diversity: How to Accept and Embrace Diversity for its Intrinsic Value

The antithesis of "managing diversity," this work enables managers to understand the *value* of diversity in terms of pragmatic business goals. Deals with the subtle and misunderstood barriers, and provides techniques to create an organization richer for its diverse nature. Equally useful as a guide for line management and as a basis for human resource professionals to build educational programs.

Doing Well by Doing Right: Guidelines for Ethical Management Practices

Why ethical management is a practical business requirement, and how to identify and eliminate ethical dilemmas. Provides insight into internal conflicts and customer conflicts, and the surprising reasons for most unethical behavior on the job. Effective for individual learning and for workshops utilizing group discussion.

Raising the Bar: Continuous Improvement As A Way of Life

How to anticipate, recognize and exploit opportunity, whether on the job or in one's personal life. Provides examples from the public and private sectors, on the small and grand scale, as to how opportunity is always knocking but few recognize the sound. Includes sources of opportunity, how to escape problem solving, and how to reward the process.

Leadership Every Day: How to Influence and Lead Others Efficiently and Effectively

Provides the range of leadership alternatives, and overcomes the focus on a "perfect style." Uses practical variables such as time management, subordinate development, commitment and quality to help determine which styles are best in what circumstances. Debunks the esoteric notions of vision and lofty mission statements, and provides practical help for leadership every day with customers, employees, vendors and the public.

Ordering information on page 51.

ALAN WEISS

Alan Weiss is the founder and president of Summit Consulting Group, Inc., a firm specializing in management and organization development. Summit's clients include organizations such as Merck & Co., Hewlett-Packard, GE, National Westminster Bank, The New York Times, Mercedes-Benz, the American Press Institute, the American Institute of Architects, Coldwell Banker and over 80 other organizations in four countries.

Alan has published over 300 articles in the fields of strategy, innovation, leadership, ethics, diversity, and interpersonal relations, in publications ranging from *Management Review* to *The New York Times.* He is the co-author of *The Innovation Formula* (1988: HarperCollins), and author of *Managing for Peak Performance* (1989: HarperCollins), *Making It Work* (1990: HarperCollins) and *Million Dollar Consulting* (1992, 1997: McGraw-Hill). His newest books are *Money Talks* (1998: McGraw-Hill) and *What Happened to Excellence* (1998: Van Nostrand). All of his books have been alternate or main book club selections, and two have been translated into German and Italian. He has also authored the Professional Development Series Booklets on major management and self-improvement topics.

He appears frequently on radio and television interview programs to discuss productivity and quality. He is a member of the American Counseling Association and the American Management Association, and is the former president of the New England Speakers Association. He holds the designation "Certified Management Consultant" from the Institute of Management Consultants, the only accrediting body requiring client references, evidence of successful engagements, and completion of a sitting examination on ethical practices. He has earned the designation "Certified Speaking Professional" from the National Speakers Association, which has recognized fewer than 300 individuals at that level of performance.

Alan is the former president of Kepner-Tregoe Continuing Education, and vice president of Kepner-Tregoe, Inc., an international training firm, and the former CEO of Walter V. Clarke Associates, a behavioral consulting firm. He holds a bachelor's degree in political science from Rutgers University, masters degrees in political science from Montclair College and psychology from California Coast University, and a doctorate in psychology from California Coast University. He has traveled to 49 countries and 48 states in the course of his career. *Success Magazine* has cited him in an editorial devoted to his work as "a worldwide expert in executive education."

He once appeared on the popular TV game show *Jeopardy*, where he lost badly in the first round to a dancing waiter from Iowa.

In addition to his worldwide consulting work, Alan Weiss presents over 50 keynote addresses and workshops annually for management conferences, trade association conventions and public symposia. For more information on his topics and availability, contact Summit Consulting Group, Inc. at the address or toll-free number on page 51.

Ordering Information

Please make your selections below and mail or fax this entire sheet to:

Summit Bookstore
Summit Consulting Group, Inc.
Box 1009
East Greenwich, RI 02818
Fax: 401/884-5068
E-Mail: summitconsultinggroupinc@compuserve.com
Or place your order via credit card using our
toll-free number: 800/766-7935.

Checks, AMEX, Visa, MasterCard, company purchase orders are welcome.

Please see the reverse side for volume orders and other information.

Books	Cost	Number	Total
Million Dollar Consulting (hard cover)	$29.00	______	$ _____
Best Laid Plans (hard cover)	$22.50	______	$ _____
Managing for Peak Performance (hard cover)	$18.00	______	$ _____
The Innovation Formula (soft cover)	$9.95	______	$ _____
Money Talks (hard cover)	$29.00	______	$ _____
What Happened to Excellence? (hard cover)	$29.00	______	$ _____
Cassettes			
The Consultant's Treasury (four tapes, two workbooks)	$119.95	______	$ _____
Booklets: The Professional Development Series			
How to Maximize Fees in Professional Services	$6.95	______	$ _____
Rejoicing in Diversity	$6.95	______	$ _____
Doing Well by Doing Right	$6.95	______	$ _____
Raising the Bar	$6.95	______	$ _____
Leadership Every Day	$6.95	______	$ _____
Volume order from reverse side			$ _____
Subtotal			$ _____
Rhode Isalnd only, add 7% sales tax			$ _____
Shipping: $3.00 per item (free shipping for three or more items)			$ _____
Total			$ _____

Payment by ❑ check ❑ purchach order, number:____________________

❑ AMEX ❑ Visa ❑ MasterCard, number:____________________ exp:____

Signature:______________________________ Phone:____________

Name:______________________________ Title:____________

Organization:______________________________

Address (City, State, Zip):______________________________

Volume discounts are available on the Professional Development Series Booklets:

Units	Price Per Unit
1-99	$6.95
100-499	$6.45
500-999	$5.95
1000+	$5.45

You may order booklets in any combination of titles. We can also provide the booklets with your organization's logo, with a custom-designed introduction, or with a preface written by a company executive. Please call for details and charges.

Please send the following booklets in the quantities specified:

Title:	Number:
How to Maximize Fees in Professional Services	_______
Rejoicing in Diversity	_______
Doing Well by Doing Right	_______
Raising the Bar	_______
Leadership Every Day	_______
Total number ordered	_______
Price per unit above	$_______
Total price (Record on reverse side)	**$________**